Recipes from our mothers are a wonderful gift. I hope you enjoy these!

R

INDIAN COOKING

FROM MY MOM

RUPEN's

www.RupenRao.com

Warren Publishing, Inc.

R

Published by Warren Publishing, Inc.
Charlotte, NC 28277
www.warrenpublishing.net

ISBN: 978-0-9894814-7-2

Library of Congress Control Number: 2013952313

Thank You

Mr. Christopher Schwalm
(Food Photographer)
Web: www.CJSchwalm.com

Ms. Pankhuri Singhal
(Content Editing)

It has been a pleasure working with both of you on this project. The enthusiasm and professionalism shown by you two has truly helped me make this book a reality. Thank you, Chris, for your excellent photography and commitment to this project, and thank you, Pankhuri, for shaping this book exactly the way I wanted it to be.

I look forward to working with you both on other projects in the future!

TABLE OF CONTENTS

MUMMY

My parents are the center of my universe. I call my dad 'Daddy' and my mom 'Mummy.' To me, Mummy is a role model of humility, simplicity, perseverance, and dedication. She is the best mom I could have had growing up and an excellent life-partner for my dad. They have now been married for 46 years! She is also an excellent cook, who not only prepares Indian cuisine but has also managed to expand her repertoire to Indian-Chinese and Western cooking (baking especially).

This book is my humble tribute to my mom; in fact, it is a collection of some of her recipes that I have managed to put together to share with everyone. When I came to the USA, my mom wrote me a book of her simple Indian recipes, and that was a great help to me when I started learning to cook over here. Thank you to my mom for sharing her recipes for me to prepare in my new home, Washington, DC.

My mom, Mrs. Shalini Rao, was born on November 21, 1942 in the city of Indore, which is located in the central state of Madhya Pradesh in India. She was born into an extremely wealthy family and was the youngest daughter amongst a total of five siblings (four sisters, one brother).

She tells me that, growing up in her home in Indore, her family had a lot of help from maids, servants, and other family members. In spite of the added help, daily chores were divided early on, right when the children entered their teens. All the children were assigned weekly tasks, including laundry, cleaning, dusting, cooking, and prepping, amongst others. Hence, learning to prep, chop, and cook was something that she learned early on in her life. Sometimes the family used to cook together, and sometimes assignments were given individually. By the tender age of 13, my mom knew all the household chores, including cooking daily meals for everyone in the family.

Apart from working on household chores, she and her other siblings went to school and worked their way to college. In the small town of Ujjain, a two-hour drive from Indore, she completed her Masters of Arts in Marathi, our native language. She then worked for a few years as a school teacher, teaching Marathi language classes in primary school.

My mom's hobbies while growing up included training in classical Indian music singing and dancing. She was an excellent dancer, performing professionally for several years in school and college.

My father first saw my mom at a dance performance during their college days. They married in 1967, when she left for the big city of Mumbai, India, where my father was stationed. They have lived there ever since.

My father did not come from an affluent family as my mom did; hence, they both had to work hard to make ends meet. In Mumbai, my mom continued her job as a school teacher. My brother was born a year after they got married. Taking care of my brother, going to school, and running the household became a full-time job for my mom. It amazes me to think about how she handled everything! Eight years later, I was born. She took a step back in her teaching career and decided to become a stay-at-home mom.

I remember, while growing up, we did not go out to eat a lot. It was only on special occasions that we ate out in restaurants. A lot of good food was made at home, and on many occasions. There were religious festivals throughout the year, for which my mom made specific food. I remember savoring all the tasty treats! Then there were birthdays, relatives and friends visiting . . . and my mom's cooked food always kept perfuming our home—each day, each week, each month, each year, for many decades.

It was not too late when I realized the power that food brings into a family; it binds a family together. A good cook in the house contributes to the health, wealth, and the over-all well-being of family members.

My friends and my neighbors always told me that I was very lucky to have a great cook as my mom! She cooked much better and healthier food than what was available in restaurants. Little Rupen could not have had it any better!

Mummy made all our meals for us every single day. Now that I think of it, it is a tedious and repetitive task to do this, and that too for a lifetime. I have so much respect for the home cook in every household. He or she puts in so much thankless effort just to keep the family together. So many breakfasts, lunches, and dinners have been made, parties and functions have been hosted, and guests have been treated—with great food!

I started helping out my mom every now and then, but I had not helped her enough. I learned a lot from watching her in the kitchen as I sat by the window while she tried exotic recipes, which were sometimes from other regions of India and sometimes international. My mom's elder sister is a fabulous cook as well. Even to this day, she caters to events in our native place in Indore. Both the sisters have entered many food-related competitions and secured first prizes. Indeed, a proud moment for the entire family.

We have been very lucky that, for the most part, we never had to cut corners or compromise on the quality of food or availability of certain expensive ingredients. Whatever was needed was provided for. However, I have seen my mom add potatoes if we did not have enough shrimp in the shrimp curry, or dice mangoes into smaller pieces if mangoes were expensive that year. I still practice these shortcuts that can help stretch my dollar. The key is to buy and prepare only what is required and never to waste any food.

As time flew by, my brother got married, and the newest addition to our family was my sister-in-law. My sister-in-law is a good cook as well, and my mom shared recipes with her so that the tradition continues. My first niece was born; I moved to the United States. A few years later, my second niece was born, and our kitchen kept delivering.

Now that my mom is 74 years old, she has taken a step back in the household. Chores, particularly food-related chores, are now taken care of by my sister-in-law and her two daughters, my two lovely nieces. It is very interesting to see the full circle of life and how everything has to come back to the place from where it began. Here in the US, I do my bit toward sharing my heritage and culture with so many people around me through my cooking classes!

All I can say is: thank you, Mummy!

MUMMY'S KITCHEN

Rasoi, the Indian kitchen, is the sacred space in our home. Here, food rules dictate the culture of our family. In our household, as in many, it is the kitchen where the altar is kept, so the kitchen serves the dual purpose of a kitchen as well as a temple inside our home.

In many homes, it is a custom to not wear footwear when in the kitchen. This is done because footwear is also generally prohibited on temple premises. The same temple rules are applicable to a kitchen with a shrine. Another reason footwear is typically not worn in the kitchen is to respect the food and treat it as a gift from God.

Mummy prepares food with love and devotion. She cooks mostly in aluminum or stainless steel pots and pans since they are long lasting. In olden times, at my grandmother's house in our native place, food was prepared in clay pots and pans. It is incredible to see how times and utensils have changed, yet the love with which food is prepared has not!

Spices

Spices form an essential ingredient in Indian cuisine. Spices are used for flavor and color. They aid in digestion as well. They contain essential oils that are good for our bodies. Mummy has her own spice mix recipes for various dishes that she makes at home. It is common in many households, where they take pride in their specific spice mix recipe, which provides a unique taste to their dishes.

In our kitchen, the Spice Box (*masala dabba*) had the essential spices. This is a common feature in all Indian kitchens. The Spice Box is a box made of stainless steel in which spices are stored, and the box is covered with a lid. '*Masala*' means 'a spice' or 'a mix of spices'; thus, frequently used spices are put in the *masala dabba* and used as required.

The Spice Box leaves the cook with a great deal of creativity. Using approximate measurements rather than measured spices, cooking becomes creative, and the flavor of a dish can be adjusted based on the amount of ingredients used. Most Spice Boxes will contain about the same ingredients, but the use of the ingredients in different quantities will make uniquely flavored dishes. Regional cooking influences the types or combinations of spices used in certain dishes.

Commonly used spices:

 Black Peppercorns – Black pepper is usually used as a whole spice in Indian cooking.

 Cumin seeds – Cumin is very much a part of Indian cuisine. This smoky spice with no heat is used in curries, pilafs, and lentils, whole or ground.

 Coriander seeds – Coriander seeds are the seeds of the coriander (cilantro) plant. Coriander seeds and ground coriander are used as the main ingredient in curry powder. This spice has a unique flavor.

 Cayenne powder / Red chili powder – Cayenne or chili powder is the backbone spice used for producing heat in Indian cuisine. A little bit goes a long way. Usually ground in curries, sometimes cayenne or chili can be used as a whole spice.

 Paprika powder / Kashmiri red chili – This spice is used mostly for coloring curries. It has little or no heat, and a good amount can be added to curries without increasing the spiciness.

Dry fenugreek leaves- Fenugreek leaves that are dry are used as an herb, especially in North Indian curries. They have a unique flavor and bitter taste. Crush dry fenugreek leaves and then add to your dish; this will enhance the flavor.

Black mustard seeds – Black mustard seeds are used largely in Indian cooking, in lentils, curries, and in rice dishes. They need to be cooked in oil. A lid is always handy because mustard seeds pop when they are cooked.

Turmeric powder – This is the mostly widely used spice in Indian cooking. It is the mother of all spices, highly antiseptic, and used for its mild flavor and strong color.

Saffron – In India, this spice comes from the Indian state of Kashmir. It is derived from a flower and is used in exotic dishes—desserts, *biryanis*, *pulao*, and sometimes in curries. It is very fragrant, and a little goes a long way.

Cardamom – Cardamom is a sweet yet potent spice. It is usually white or green pods with black or brown seeds in them, all of which are edible. It is used whole in rice dishes and curries and as a ground spice in desserts.

Cinnamon sticks – In Indian cooking, cinnamon is used whole. It is the outermost bark of the Cassia tree; thus, the tree need not be chopped down to derive cinnamon. Since it is the outermost bark of the tree, it is much stronger in flavor than the cinnamon found in the West.

Bay leaves – Bay leaves are used in curries and rice dishes. They are used as a dry leaf, which is much stronger than the fresh bay leaf. When the meal is served, the bay leaf is served as well. You must discard the bay leaf, as it is not edible.

 Cloves – Cloves are used as a whole spice in Indian cooking. They are used in lentils, rice dishes, and curries. This spice has a strong flavor, and cloves and clove oil is known to strengthen gums.

 Curry powder – It is not one spice; instead, it is a mix of three main spices: turmeric, coriander, and cumin. If you do not have curry powder, I suggest adding each of the key ingredients individually.

 ***Garam masala* powder** – This spice blend is a mix of warm spices such as black cardamom, black pepper, cinnamon, bay leaves, cloves, and many more. It is a combination of spices used in Indian cooking. '*Garam*' means 'spicy' and '*masala*' means 'a spice mix'; hence, the term '*garam masala*' means simply 'a mix of spices.'

Other spices that are part of Indian cooking are black cardamom pods, fenugreek seeds, fennel seeds, star anise, carom seeds, and caraway seeds. Different combinations of these spices will result in distinct flavors that are invariably part of Indian cuisine.

Special Tools

Indian cooking involves using special tools, some of which are unique to our cooking methods, which make cooking convenient and pragmatic and minimize effort to a certain extent. Some of these tools that are used by Mummy in our kitchen back home:

1. **Mortar and Pestle** – Indian cooking uses a lot of spices and chutneys, and this tool is used to grind spices and ingredients for chutneys, such as garlic and ginger.

2. **Wok (*kadhai*)** – A *kadhai* is an Indian wok, usually made of aluminum, and can hold up to 4 quarts. The *kadhai* is a must in homes all over India. Modern day *kadhai*s are made of stainless steel or are non-stick. A sauté pan is a good substitute.

3. **Tools to prepare Indian breads (*paraat, chakla* & *belan*)** – These three tools are used to make the dough for Indian breads. A *paraat* is a copper or stainless steel plate that is about 2 feet wide and is deeper than a regular plate. Flour is added to the *paraat*, and dough is kneaded in it. The *chakla* is the surface tool that is used to roll breads and the *belan* is the rolling pin. These tools differ in shape and size from the ones that we find in the West.

4. **Pressure cooker** – This time-saving device is used to cook lentils and tough red meat that otherwise require long hours of cooking. It is usually made out of aluminum but can be found in non-stick varieties as well. Since Indian cuisine is heavily based on beans and lentils, this device is a must in all Indian homes.

5. **Blender and a food chopper** – A blender is used to make chutneys, soups, and pastes. A food chopper is used to grind onions, ginger, garlic, coconut, chilies, etc. They are both extensively used in Indian cooking.

Techniques to use ingredients in Indian Cooking

Many of us find it difficult to understand the ways of Indian cooking. Indian cooking, like any other cuisine, has its own nuances, details and techniques. I am sharing some of them so that it will help you cook Indian food the way it is prepared in homes in India.

Curry leaves – Curry leaves are extensively used in South Indian cooking. These leaves from the Kadi plant (*Kadi patta*) have a fresh lemony flavor. Rinse and pat dry curry leaves, wrap in paper towels and refrigerate. Use within a couple of weeks for best results.

Onion – Onions must always be medium-size red onions, unless the recipe specifically calls otherwise. They should not be too tiny or too large, for the flavor of the onion differs with size. Mincing the onion is the key to making good curries.

Ginger and garlic – Garlic is always peeled, and ginger with the skin on is perfectly fine. Rinse, dry and mince. Finely chopped ginger and garlic are acceptable as well.

Whole spices – Whole spices are treated differently from their ground-up versions. Cooking the spices is very important. Whole spices are added directly to hot oil, and they perfume the oil when being sautéed during initial cooking. Ground spices are NOT added directly to hot oil as they will burn. They are added later in the process of cooking.

Muddling – Sometimes whole spices will need to be partially crushed; I refer to this as 'muddling.' I use a mortar and pestle to muddle my spices, for just half a minute. This brings out essential oils and perfumes the dish immediately.

Cilantro – Cilantro is used as a garnish in savory dishes. Cilantro is added only as a garnish as cooking it will make it wilt and discolor.

Green peas – Frozen green peas are your best bet. They are partially cooked and convenient. Add them during the latter part of cooking a dish, and they will thaw with the heat in the curry/ rice and will not discolor.

Jalapeño or green chili – A quarter of a jalapeño is a perfect substitute for one small green chili. Jalapeño veins and seeds are used in cooking since that's where all the heat of the pepper lies. Do not discard veins and seeds.

Black mustard seeds must only be added when the oil is hot. Once added, you must wait for them to crackle and then for the crackling to somewhat stop. If you do not, then black mustard seeds may add bitterness to your lentils.

Beans – If you are soaking beans in water, then make sure you pour the soaked water on to plants since some bean nutrition has dissolved into the water in which the beans were soaked. If you are using canned beans (garbanzo or red kidney beans), then rinse beans thoroughly before adding them to your dish.

Specific Indian ingredients

Fresh shredded coconut - Indian stores carry a frozen pack of fresh coconut that is scraped. This is a popular ingredient in Indian cooking. Coconut milk is a substitute, but the taste of fresh coconut is way better than using canned coconut milk.

Curry leaves - Curry leaves are extensively used in South Indian and Coastal Indian cuisine. They have a lemony flavor and are generally sautéed in oil or *ghee*. They are used as a tempering for lentils or as part of curries.

Dried mango powder - This ingredient is a ground mixture of mangoes that have been dried. It is sour and hence used as a souring agent in curries.

Tamarind - Tamarind is a sour tropical fruit, the pulp of which is used as a souring agent in Indian cooking.

Asafetida – Asafetida (or *hing*) is a crystal-like substance (also available in powder form) that is used as a digestive in Indian cooking. It is added to dishes that are high in protein.

Ghee – *Ghee* is clarified butter that is made from cow's milk. It can also be made by cooking unsalted butter. It is used in lentils, desserts and rice. It has a higher smoking point than butter and is liquid when heated. At room temperature, *ghee* is opaque and solid.

Poppadums – *Poppadums* are lentil wafers, made from various lentils; sometimes they are a mix of lentil dough and black pepper. They are referred to as '*papad*' and are used as an accompaniment in a meal. They can be roasted over heat or deep fried.

Jaggery – *Jaggery*, usually obtained from boiling sugarcane juice, is unrefined sugar that contains beneficial minerals. It is used as a healthier option to refined white sugar.

CHUTNEYS, RAITAS & SALADS

An Indian meal is always accompanied by some kind of fresh chutney, salad and/or *raita*. Chutney is typically a combination of fresh herbs, fruits, or nuts that has been mashed with some spices. *Raita* is a yogurt-based accompaniment that can be sweet or savory, with some or no spices added to it.

In Indian cooking, salads are usually onions, carrots or green chilies that are sliced and served along with the entrée. Mummy makes one lightly seasoned salad.

Peanut Chutney
Moongphali ki Chutney

Serves: **4** | Time to prepare: **15 minutes** | Store: **Refrigerator, for one week**

Ingredients

1 cup roasted peanuts, skinless
1 teaspoon cumin seeds
2 garlic cloves
½ teaspoon salt
1 teaspoon sugar
¼ teaspoon turmeric powder
1 Tablespoon chopped cilantro

Instructions

1. In a food chopper, add all the ingredients except cilantro. Grind coarsely.
2. Remove from blender in a mixing bowl and add cilantro, mix, and serve.

Fresh Coconut Chutneys
Nariyal ki Chutney

Coconut chutney has many variations. Here, I have mentioned three kinds that Mummy makes. Traditionally, you make the chutney and then pour 'tempering' ingredients on it and mix well. Use fresh coconut for this chutney; it is found in the frozen section at the Indian, Asian, or Latin stores.

Serves: **4** | Time to prepare: **15 minutes** | Store: **Refrigerator, for 3–4 days**

1) Coconut Chutney – 1 cup grated fresh coconut
2) Coconut and Peanut Chutney – ½ cup grated fresh coconut AND ½ cup peanuts
3) Coconut and Dal Chutney – ½ cup grated fresh coconut AND ½ cup split yellow peas (roasted)

Once you have any one of the above three combinations, here is the recipe:

Ingredients

Blend:
One of the above combinations along with
2 Tablespoons full fat plain yogurt
1 teaspoon cumin seeds
½ teaspoon salt
1 teaspoon black mustard seeds
1 jalapeño, roughly chopped

Tempering:

1 Tablespoon oil
½ teaspoon black mustard seeds
½ teaspoon cumin seeds
2 pinches of asafetida powder (*hing*) (OPTIONAL)
1 dry red chili, broken in 2
3 curry leaves, each torn in 2 pieces (OPTIONAL)
Salt, to taste

Instructions

1. Using a food chopper (like Magic Bullet) or a blender, puree all the ingredients on the 'Blend' setting. Empty into a small mixing bowl and set aside.
2. In a small fry pan over medium heat, heat oil. When the oil is hot, add mustard seeds and allow crackling. Keep a lid handy.
3. When the crackling has stopped, add cumin seeds, asafetida, dry red chili, and curry leaves, and cook for a minute.
4. Add this mixture to the freshly prepared chutney. Add salt and mix. Chutney is ready to serve along with your entrée.

Tomato Chutney
Tamatar ki Chutney

Serves: **4–6** | Time to prepare: **60 minutes** | Store: **Refrigerator, for 3–4 days**

Mummy makes this chutney when tomatoes are in abundance and on sale. The key is to slow cook tomatoes to let them pulp; therefore, a little bit of patience is required. Serve cold along with roti or rice—a perfect accompaniment.

Ingredients

3 Tablespoons oil
1 teaspoon black mustard seeds
1 teaspoon cumin seeds
½ teaspoon asafetida (*hing*)
    OPTIONAL
4-5 curry leaves, each torn into two
    OPTIONAL
1 Tablespoon fresh ginger, minced
1 Tablespoon peeled garlic, minced
½ jalapeño, finely chopped
½ teaspoon turmeric powder
1 teaspoon salt, OR as desired
4 cups finely chopped large Roma
    tomatoes
1 teaspoon white sugar OR *jaggery*

Instructions

1. Heat oil in a 3-qt. sauce-pan over medium heat.
2. When the oil is hot, add mustard seeds and allow crackling. Then add cumin seeds, curry leaves (if using), and asafetida. Sauté for a minute.
3. Then add ginger, garlic, and chopped jalapeños. Cook for 2–3 minutes.
4. Add turmeric powder, salt, and tomatoes. Mix well and cook covered on low heat for 30–40 minutes, stirring every 5 minutes or so. Finally add sugar or *jaggery* and stir. Cook for another couple of minutes.
5. Let cool, then refrigerate. Serve cold or at room temperature as chutney.

Sesame Chutney
Til ki Chutney

Ingredients

1 cup white sesame seeds
2 garlic cloves
½ teaspoon salt
1 teaspoon sugar
¼ teaspoon turmeric powder

Instructions

1. In a small fry pan over medium heat, lightly roast sesame seeds for 5 minutes. Stir constantly. Set aside to cool.
2. In a food chopper, add all the ingredients along with sesame seeds and grind.
3. Remove from food chopper into a mixing bowl and serve.

Poppadum Chutney
Papad ki Chutney

Ingredients

2 black pepper *poppadums*, roasted
1 Tablespoon light oil
¼ teaspoon cayenne powder
¼ teaspoon turmeric powder
Salt, a couple of pinches

Instructions

1. Crush roasted *poppadums* so that there is a coarse mixture. Set aside.
2. In a medium fry pan over medium heat, heat oil. When the oil is hot, add crushed *poppadums*, salt, cayenne, and turmeric, and mix. Sauté for 2–3 minutes, and the chutney is ready to serve.

Both chutneys: Serves: **4–6** | Time to prepare: **15 minutes** | Store: **Refrigerator, for 3–4 days**

INDIAN COOKING FROM MY MOM

Green Chutney
Dhaniya aur Pudinay ki Chutney

Ingredients

1 bunch rinsed & chopped cilantro
  (including stalk; just trim the last 1")
½ cup mint leaves, chopped
2 tablespoons lemon juice
½ jalapeño OR as desired
1 teaspoon sugar
1 Tablespoon cumin seeds
Salt, to taste

Instructions

In a blender (not a food processor) or a
food chopper, blend all the ingredients
with little or no water and form a paste.
Serve as an accompaniment.

Serves: **4–6** | Time to prepare: **15 minutes** | Store: **Refrigerator, for 3–4 days**

Chickpea Chutney
Chana Dal Chutney

Ingredients

1 cup split chickpea lentils
½ teaspoon salt
1 teaspoon sugar
¼ teaspoon cayenne powder

Tempering.
2 Tablespoons oil
1 teaspoon black mustard seeds
1 teaspoon cumin seeds
¼ teaspoon turmeric powder

Instructions

1. In a mixing bowl, soak lentils in 1 cup water for 4 hours. Discard water after 4 hours.
2. Grind lentils in a food chopper.
3. Remove into a mixing bowl. Add salt, sugar, and cayenne. Mix well and set aside.
4. In a small fry pan over medium heat, heat oil. Add mustard seeds and allow crackling.
5. Then add cumin seeds and turmeric powder. Remove from heat. Add this mixture to the ground lentils and mix. Serve.

Serves: **4–6** | Time to prepare: **4 hours** (includes soaking time) |
Store: **Refrigerator, for 3–4 days**

Dry Coconut Chutney
Sookhay Nariyal ki Chutney

Ingredients

1 cup dry unsweetened shredded coconut
½ teaspoon salt
1/8 teaspoon cayenne powder

Tempering.
2 Tablespoons oil
1 teaspoon black mustard seeds
1 teaspoon cumin seeds
¼ jalapeño, minced
¼ teaspoon turmeric powder

Instructions

1. In a medium mixing bowl, mix coconut, salt, and cayenne. Set aside.
2. In a small fry pan, heat oil over medium heat.
3. Add mustard seeds and allow crackling.
4. Add cumin and jalapeño. Sauté for a minute.
5. Add turmeric powder and remove from heat. Add this mixture to the coconut mixture and stir.

Serves: **4–6** | Time to prepare: **15 minutes** |
Store: **Refrigerator, for 3–4 days**

Lightly Seasoned Vegetable Salad

Koshimbir

Serves: **4** | Time to prepare: **30 minutes** | Store: **Refrigerator, for 3–4 days**

Indian cuisine does not include salad as a course. The only salad ingredient one sees is the inclusion of raw onion, raw carrots, and raw green chilies on the plate. One of the most popular ones, from the state of Maharashtra, is *koshimbir* (or *kachumbar* as it is known in Hindi).

Ingredients

1 red onion, finely chopped, enough to make 1 cup
2 Roma tomatoes, finely chopped, enough to make 1 cup
½ cup grated cauliflower
1 teaspoon oil
½ teaspoon mustard seeds
½ teaspoon cumin seeds
¼ teaspoon turmeric powder
½ teaspoon cayenne powder OR as desired
1 teaspoon sugar OR 1 teaspoon honey
Salt, to taste

Instructions

1. Mix onions, tomatoes, and cauliflower in a medium mixing bowl. Set aside.
2. Heat oil in a small pan. When hot, add mustard seeds and allow them to crackle.
3. Add cumin seeds, turmeric, and cayenne; mix in the onion-cauliflower-tomato mixture.
4. Mix well and turn off the heat. Add sugar and salt. Mix and serve.

Pineapple Raita
Ananas ka Raita

Both my nieces in Mumbai love upside-down Pineapple Cake, for which they will buy canned pineapples. Usually there are one or two pieces left for Mummy to make this *raita*. She will add leftover canned juice to this *raita* so it gets just the right additional sweetness and consistency.

Ingredients

1 cup pineapple, chopped into ½"cubes
1 cup plain yogurt
1 teaspoon cumin seeds, muddled
2 Tablespoons finely chopped cilantro
1 Tablespoon granulated sugar

Instructions

1. Mix all ingredients in a bowl.
2. Refrigerate for 1 hour and *raita* is ready to serve.

Both *raitas*. Serves: **4** | Time to prepare: **15 minutes** | Store: **Refrigerator, for 3–4 days**

Cucumber Raita
Kakdi ka Raita

Ingredients

1 cup English seedless cucumber, grated, with skin on
1 cup plain yogurt
1 Tablespoon sugar

Instructions

1. Mix all ingredients in a bowl.
2. Refrigerate for 1 hour and *raita* is ready to serve.

INDIAN COOKING FROM MY MOM

Vegetable Raita
Pyaaz, Tamatar aur Kakdi ka Raita

Ingredients

½ cup Roma tomato, chopped
½ cup seedless English cucumber, chopped
    OR ½ cup green pepper, chopped
½ cup red onion, chopped
1 cup plain low-fat yogurt
¼ jalapeño, finely chopped
¼ cup cilantro, finely chopped
1 teaspoon sugar (OPTIONAL)
½ teaspoon salt

Instructions

1. Mix all ingredients in a medium-size mixing bowl. Refrigerate.

Fried Chickpea Balls Raita
Boondi Raita

Ingredients

1 cup plain low-fat yogurt
½ cup plain *boondi* (fried chickpea balls)
½ teaspoon salt
2 teaspoons sugar
1 Tablespoon cilantro, finely chopped
½ teaspoon cumin seeds, partially crushed
¼ teaspoon cayenne powder
½ teaspoon freshly grated ginger

Instructions

1. Mix all ingredients in a medium-size mixing bowl. Refrigerate.

Both *raitas*. Serves: **4** | Time to prepare: **15 minutes** | Store: **Refrigerator, for 3–4 days**

VEGETABLES

Usage, Storage and Preparation

Vegetables are used greatly in Indian cooking since our cuisine is primarily vegetarian. There are countless recipes on preparing these vegetables that are handed down over generations. Each family takes pride in its version of preparing these recipes.

Mummy buys fresh vegetables from local markets, similar to farmer's markets over here in the US. She will prepare the vegetables within a few days of buying them. She usually stores them in the refrigerator so that they last longer.

Vegetables are bought based on the season. Certain vegetables like carrots, green peas, and corn are quite seasonal, so you may not see them throughout the year. Mummy will shell green peas and freeze them so that she can use them as and when required throughout the year. Other vegetables are cooked only during the particular season they grow in.

I have learned from Mummy that the trick to preparing a good vegetable dish lies in how well the vegetables are chopped. For example, Mummy never uses a knife to chop cauliflower florets; she uses her hands to break the florets so that they retain their shape. With cabbage, she makes sure to spend plenty of time in chopping cabbage; this is essential.

One way of preparing vegetables is to make a vegetable curry. Vegetables are sautéed along with certain spices. They are served along with lentils and bread or rice.

Sautéed Spinach with Tomatoes
Palak ki Sookhi Subzi

This recipe is an ode to simplicity. Using only a few ingredients, this recipe is packed with nutrients and flavor. Mummy uses minced garlic for this recipe; however, I prefer thinly sliced garlic. I use olive oil, but any vegetable oil can be substituted.

Serves: **4** | Time to prepare: **15 minutes** | Store: **Refrigerator, for 3–4 days**

Ingredients

2 Tablespoons olive oil
1 teaspoon cumin seeds
4 cloves garlic, peeled, finely chopped
2 dry red chilies, each broken into two
1 lb. baby spinach leaves, rinsed and pat-dried
2 Roma tomatoes, finely chopped
Salt, to taste

Instructions

1. In a 3-qt. sauté pan over medium heat, heat oil. When the oil is hot, add cumin seeds, garlic, and red chilies, and sauté for a minute.
2. Add spinach leaves and stir, mixing well, and cook for 4–5 minutes, stirring every minute.
3. When spinach has wilted, add tomatoes and sprinkle some salt. Stir.
4. Cook for 10 minutes, stirring every other minute. Serve hot.

Dry Preparation of Potatoes & Onions
Aloo aur Pyaaz subzi

Caramelized onions add a delicate sweetness to this recipe. It takes time and patience to caramelize onions. The trick is to cook potatoes without adding a drop of water. If your onions or potatoes start burning, then Mummy tells me that you can always add ¼ cup of water while potatoes are being cooked—no one will ever know!

Serves: **4** | Time to prepare: **30 minutes** | Store: **Refrigerator, for 3–4 days**

Ingredients

4 Tablespoons vegetable oil
1 Tablespoon cumin seeds
½ jalapeño, finely chopped
3 cups sliced red onions
3 medium Idaho potatoes rinsed and sliced
   into ¼" pieces, skin on
Salt, to taste

Instructions

1. In a 5-qt. wide sauté pan over medium heat, heat oil. Add cumin seeds and sauté for half a minute. Then add jalapeño and sliced onions. Sauté for 3 minutes.
2. Place potatoes on the onions, making sure they are not stacked on each other as far as possible.
3. Reduce heat to low and cook covered for 15 minutes. Check to see if the potatoes are done. If so, add salt and stir gently.
4. If not, then add ¼ cup of water and cook for 10 minutes. Adjust salt and serve hot.

Sautéed Okra
Bhindi ki Sookhi Subzi

This is a simple recipe for okra. Mummy makes various kinds of okra dishes, but this is a good recipe for a beginner.

Serves: **4** | Time to prepare: **30 minutes** | Store: **Refrigerator, for 3–4 days**

Ingredients

2 Tablespoons oil
1 teaspoon black mustard seeds
1 teaspoon cumin seeds
½ cup red onion, finely chopped
2 cups fresh okra, top trimmed and each okra chopped length-wise
1 cup Roma tomato, chopped
½ teaspoon turmeric powder
¼ teaspoon cayenne powder
Salt, to taste

Instructions

1. In a 3-qt. sauté pan over medium heat, heat oil, and add black mustard seeds. Allow mustard seeds to crackle. When the crackling has stopped, add cumin and sauté for a minute.
2. Add onions and sauté for 5 minutes, stirring every minute.
3. Add okra and sprinkle some salt. Cook covered for 15 minutes, stirring every 5 minutes.
4. Add turmeric, cayenne and tomato, mix, and cook covered for 5 minutes. Sprinkle salt and serve.

Sautéed Cabbage
Patta Gobi Sookhi Subzi

There are several ways to prepare Spicy Cabbage; this is the way Mummy makes it at home most often. The key is to take your time finely chopping the cabbage.

Serves: **4** | Time to prepare: **20 minutes** | Store: **Refrigerator, for 3–4 days**

Ingredients

2 Tablespoons olive oil
1 teaspoon cumin seeds
2 dry red chilies, each broken into two
4 cups cabbage, finely chopped
½ teaspoon turmeric powder
1 cup fresh grated coconut (SUBSTITUTE: dry unsweetened grated coconut)
2 Tablespoons finely chopped cilantro
Salt, to taste

Instructions

1. In a 3-qt. saucepan over medium heat, heat oil. When the oil is hot, add cumin seeds and red chilies and sauté for a minute.
2. Add cabbage and salt. Mix well. Add turmeric powder and mix again. Cook covered on low heat for 10 minutes. Stir once in between.
3. Add coconut and cilantro. Mix. Cook covered for another 5 minutes. Serve hot.

Spicy Cauliflower & Peas
Gobi aur Matar ki Subzi

Mummy is careful here in the way she prepares the cauliflower. Try not to use a knife to break cauliflower florets, but use your hands instead. This way they will retain their tree-like shape. If you are using frozen peas instead, then add them towards the end since they don't need to be cooked.

Serves: **4** | Time to prepare: **30 minutes** | Store: **Refrigerator, for 3–4 days**

Ingredients

2 Tablespoons oil
½ cup red onion, finely chopped
¼ jalapeño, finely chopped
1 cup Roma tomato, finely chopped
¼ teaspoon cayenne powder (OPTIONAL)
1 Tablespoon coriander powder
½ teaspoon turmeric powder
1 teaspoon *garam masala* powder
2 cups cauliflower florets, broken into 1" pieces
1 cup fresh green peas
Salt, to taste
2 Tablespoons chopped cilantro

Instructions

1. In a 5-qt. wide sauté pan over medium heat, heat oil. When the oil is hot, add onions and sauté for 5 minutes, stirring every minute.
2. Add jalapeño, tomatoes, and all the spice powders. Cook for 5 minutes. Stir every minute.
3. Add cauliflower and peas, sprinkle some salt, and mix.
4. Reduce heat to low and cook covered for 15 minutes, stirring every 5 minutes.
5. Garnish with cilantro and serve.

Pumpkin & Fresh Coconut
Kaddu aur Nariyal ki Subzi

This is the only way we like pumpkin in our house. Each year, this recipe is made several times! I have another recipe for pumpkin, a soup recipe. I shared my pumpkin soup recipe with Mummy, which I learned from my friend Haley, who I think is the best cook I have met in Washington, DC!

When you prepare pumpkin for this recipe, you can always wash the seeds and toast them in the oven for 15 minutes at 350° F. Once cooled, shell and eat the inside of pumpkin seeds.

Serves: **4** | Time to prepare: **45 minutes** | Store: **Refrigerator, for 3-4 days**

Ingredients

2 Tablespoons vegetable oil
2 pinches *hing* (asafetida) (OPTIONAL)
1 teaspoon black mustard seeds
1 Tablespoon cumin seeds
5–6 curry leaves, each torn in two pieces
¼ jalapeño, finely chopped
1 lb. pumpkin, deseeded, peeled and cubed into 1" pieces
¼ cup fresh coconut, shredded
Salt, to taste
¼ cup chopped cilantro
1 Tablespoon freshly squeezed lemon juice

Instructions

1. In a 5-qt. wide sauté pan (preferably non-stick) over medium heat, heat oil. When the oil is hot, add hing and black mustard seeds and allow mustard seeds to crackle.
2. When the crackling has stopped, add cumin seeds, jalapeño, and curry leaves. Sauté for 2 minutes.
3. Add pumpkin and sprinkle some salt, mix well. Reduce heat to low and cook covered for 25 minutes, stirring every 5 minutes.
4. Garnish with coconut and cilantro. Add lemon juice. Mix again. Serve.

Green Peppers cooked with Chickpea Flour
Shimla Mirch aur Besan ki Subzi

My friend Ari's mom gave me this recipe; she made it once when I was visiting her and Ari in New Jersey. Ever since, I've made green peppers just like this. Mummy also makes them the exact same way, but I had no idea until I shared this recipe with her.

Serves: **4** | Time to prepare: **30 minutes** | Store: **Refrigerator, for 3–4 days**

Ingredients

2 Tablespoons vegetable oil
1 teaspoon cumin seeds
¼ jalapeño, finely chopped
½ cup chickpea flour
4 bell peppers, chopped into 2"
   cubes
Salt, to taste

Spice Mix:
1 Tablespoon coriander powder
½ teaspoon turmeric powder
1 teaspoon mango powder
¼ teaspoon cayenne powder
½ teaspoon *garam masala* powder

Instructions

1. In a 3-qt. sauté pan over medium heat, heat oil and add cumin seeds and jalapeño. Sauté for 2 minutes, then add chickpea flour. Cook for 5 minutes; stirring every minute.
2. Add green peppers and sprinkle some salt. Mix. Cook covered for 10 minutes; stir every other minute.
3. Add spice powders and mix. Cook covered for another 5 minutes. Serve.

Sautéed Dill

Sooa ki Sookhi Subzi

This is the dry preparation of dill, Indian style. After moving to the US, I have fallen in love with this green vegetable. If you find the flavor of dill overpowering, then it is a good idea to add a cup of fresh spinach leaves to this dish to balance out the strong flavor.

Serves: **4** | Time to prepare: **30 minutes** | Store: **Refrigerator, for 3–4 days**

Ingredients

¼ cup mung lentils, soaked in 1 cup water for 30 minutes
2 Tablespoons oil
2 pinches *hing* (asafetida)
2 dry red chilies, each broken into two
3–4 garlic cloves, peeled and thinly sliced
2 cups dill, chopped
Salt, to taste

Instructions

1. In a 3-qt. sauté pan over medium heat, heat oil and add *hing*, red chilies, and garlic cloves. Sauté for 2 minutes.
2. Add mung lentils along with the soaking water.
3. Add dill and sprinkle some salt. Mix.
4. Cover and cook on low heat for 25 minutes. Serve.

French-Cut Beans cooked with Fresh Coconut

Beans Foogath

Serves: **4** | Time to prepare: **30 minutes** | Store: **Refrigerator, for 3–4 days**

Ingredients

2 Tablespoons vegetable oil
1 teaspoon black mustard seeds
1 teaspoon cumin seeds
7–8 curry leaves, each torn into two
1 dry red chili, torn into two
2 cups frozen French-cut beans, thawed
2 Tablespoons fresh coconut
   (SUBSTITUTE: 2 Tablespoons dry unsweetened coconut)
Salt, to taste

Instructions

1. In a 3-qt. sauté pan over medium heat, heat oil and add black mustard seeds. Allow crackling. When the crackling has stopped, add dry red chili and cumin seeds.
2. Add curry leaves and sauté for half a minute.
3. Add beans and sprinkle some salt. Cook covered for 15 minutes, stirring every 5 minutes.
4. Add coconut, mix, and serve.

Potatoes & Peas Curry
Aloo Matar

This curry is served in all temples in India.

Serves: **4** | Time to prepare: **30 minutes** | Store: **Refrigerator, for 3-4 days**

Ingredients

2 Tablespoons *ghee*
1 teaspoon white poppy seeds
2–3 green cardamoms, partially crushed
2 teaspoons fresh garlic, peeled and finely
   chopped
1 teaspoon fresh ginger, peeled and finely
   chopped
½ cup red onion, finely chopped
1 teaspoon turmeric powder
1 teaspoon cayenne powder
1 teaspoon *garam masala*
1 cup Roma tomatoes, cubed
2 cups Idaho potatoes, boiled, peeled and
   chopped into 1" cubes
1 cup frozen green peas
Salt, to taste
1 teaspoon mango powder
1 Tablespoon cilantro, finely chopped

Instructions

1. In a 5-qt. sauté pan over medium heat,
   add *ghee*. Once hot, add white poppy
   seeds and cardamom pods. Sauté for 1
   minute, then add ginger and garlic.
   Sauté for 1 minute.
2. Add onions and sauté till pink. Add spice
   powders and tomatoes. Cook for 5
   minutes or until tomatoes become
   tender.
3. Add 1 cup water and potatoes. Cook for
   approximately 10 minutes.
4. Add green peas and salt. Garnish with
   cilantro and serve hot.

Smoked & Pureed Eggplant Curry
Baingan Bharta

'*Baingan*' means 'eggplant' and '*bharta*' means 'to mash.' This is a recipe from the north of India. Charring the eggplant on a gas burner is the key to this recipe. It is then that you get the smokiness in this dish.

Serves: **4** | Time to prepare: **30 minutes** | Store: **Refrigerator, for 3–4 days**

Ingredients

2 medium-size eggplants
2 Tablespoons vegetable oil
1 cup minced red onion
½ jalapeño, finely chopped
1 teaspoon chopped fresh ginger
1 teaspoon finely chopped fresh peeled garlic
1 cup finely chopped Roma tomatoes
2 Tablespoons cilantro, chopped
1 Tablespoon lemon juice
Salt, to taste

Spice Mix.
1 Tablespoon curry powder
1 teaspoon *garam masala* powder
1 teaspoon paprika powder
¼ teaspoon cayenne powder

Instructions

1. Place eggplant directly over medium heat on a gas stove, cook for 3 minutes and turn over, using a pair of tongs. Repeat until all 4 sides are cooked. Remove from heat and place on a dish and set aside to cool. If you do not have a gas stove, then pre-heat oven at 400°F and bake eggplant for 45 minutes. Remove and place on a dish.
2. Remove eggplant skin and mash eggplant.
3. Meanwhile, in a 3-qt. sauté pan, heat oil over medium heat. When the oil is hot, sauté onions and jalapeño until onions begin to caramelize. Stir once every minute.
4. Add ginger and garlic. Sauté for 5 minutes.
5. Add tomatoes and ground spices, stir. Cover and cook for 5 minutes, stirring once after 3 minutes.
6. Add eggplant to the onion mixture. Stir. Adjust salt and cook for 5 minutes.
7. Garnish with cilantro and sprinkle lemon juice. Serve hot.

INDIAN COOKING FROM MY MOM

Spinach & Paneer Curry
Palak Paneer

'*Palak*' means 'spinach' and '*paneer*' is the Indian cottage cheese. Mummy sometimes deep fries the *paneer* before adding it to this recipe. I usually don't do that though, simply to keep this recipe light and healthy.

Serves: **4** | Time to prepare: **30 minutes** | Store: **Refrigerator, for 3–4 days**

Ingredients

4 cups baby spinach leaves
1 inch fresh ginger
2 Tablespoons *ghee*
1 Tablespoon cumin seeds
¼ jalapeno, finely chopped
3–4 garlic cloves, peeled and chopped
1 cup red onion, finely chopped
1 cup Roma tomato, finely chopped
1 teaspoon *garam masala* powder
1 cup *paneer*, chopped into 1" cubes
Salt, to taste
1 Tablespoon lemon juice

Instructions

1. In a 3-qt. sauté pan, boil 4 cups water. When the water comes to a boil, add spinach and ginger. Cook for 5 minutes.
2. Strain using a colander and puree cooked spinach and ginger in a blender.
3. In a 3-qt. sauté pan, melt *ghee* and add cumin seeds, jalapeño, and garlic. Cook for a minute. Add onions and sauté for 7 minutes, stirring every minute.
4. Add tomatoes and *garam masala* powder.
5. Add pureed spinach and sprinkle some salt. Reduce heat to low as spinach may splutter; also have a lid handy. Mix.
6. Add *paneer* pieces and stir gently. Cook partially covered for 5 minutes. Add lemon juice and serve with Indian bread or rice.

Note: When cooking spinach, do not cover the pot with a lid or spinach will discolor.

INDIAN COOKING FROM MY MOM

SEAFOOD, POULTRY & LAMB

Usage, Storage, and Preparation

USAGE:

Seafood and poultry in India is brought fresh from the market and cooked the very same day. I remember as a child, I used to hate entering the fish market. My dad used to go buy non-vegetarian products in the morning when he took our dog for a walk. We cooked non-vegetarian food only once a week, and it was almost always a Sunday—Sunday because everyone has a day off and the entire family can eat together.

STORAGE:

Once cooked, non-vegetarian food is eaten right after it has been prepared. If there are leftovers, they are refrigerated and consumed later that day or the next day. Meat is never frozen since electricity fluctuates a lot in all parts of India and there is never a guarantee that the meat will be preserved properly.

PREPARATION:

When I was growing up, shrimp was never sold shelled or deveined. The tedious task of shelling and deveining shrimp was done by Mummy. This took quite some time. Chicken or goat meat, although cleaned, was always sold bone-in; it was cooked bone-in as well. Cooking meat with bones will add more flavors, but these days, for the sake of convenience, we prefer boneless meat. Skin was always discarded since it is all fat to begin with.

In Indian cooking, non-vegetarian food is always over-cooked. Since it is mostly cooked in a curry, it does not dry out, and overcooking ensures safety in consuming meat. No edible part is wasted.

Masala Scrambled Eggs
Anday ki Bhurji

Indian-style scrambled eggs are very popular in every household. Some recipes call for adding ginger and garlic, but Mummy keeps it simple. This is also street-food in India.

Serves: **4** | Time to prepare: **30 minutes** | Store: **Refrigerator, for 2 days**

Ingredients

4 eggs, broken and whisked
2 Tablespoons vegetable oil
2 cups red onion, minced
¼ jalapeño, minced
1 cup Roma tomato, finely chopped
¼ teaspoon cayenne powder
½ teaspoon turmeric powder
Salt, to taste

Instructions

1. Heat oil in a 3-qt. sauté pan and add jalapeño and onions. Sauté for 10 minutes, stirring every minute.
2. Add tomato and cook for 5 minutes.
3. Add the remaining ingredients, including a couple of pinches of salt along with eggs, to the sauté pan. Stir continuously for 3 minutes.
4. Reduce heat to low and keep crumbling the egg mixture until eggs are cooked. Garnish with cilantro.

Pan Fried Fish
Garam Masala Machchli Fry

This fish fry is simple and delicious. If you are health-conscious and would not want to fry fish in oil, then you can bake it in a pre-heated oven at 350° F for about 20 minutes.

Serves: **4** | Time to prepare: **30 minutes** | Store: **Refrigerator, for 2 days**

Ingredients

Spice Mix:
½ cup semolina
1 Tablespoon salt
1 teaspoon cayenne powder
1 Tablespoon *garam masala* powder
1 teaspoon turmeric powder
1 Tablespoon paprika powder

½ cup vegetable oil
3 Tilapia fillets, each fillet cut in 5 equal pieces
2 lemons, quartered

Instructions

1. In a medium mixing bowl, mix the 'Spice Mix' ingredients.
2. Heat oil in a medium fry pan over medium heat.
3. Meanwhile, dunk tilapia pieces (one at a time) in the spice mixture, dust, and set aside. Repeat this process for all pieces.
4. When the oil is hot, shallow fry 3 pieces at a time, for 3 minutes on each side. Remove and place on a paper towel to absorb excess oil.
5. Squeeze lemon juice and serve hot.
6. Wait until the oil gets hot again, and repeat frying fish pieces.

Note: If you need more oil to shallow fry some of the pieces, then you can always add ¼ cup vegetable oil to the fry pan. Wait until the oil gets hot and continue shallow frying.

Sautéed Dried Shrimp
Sukha Jhinga

Mummy makes this only occasionally; my parents and I love this dried shrimp dish. It is a side dish and when you cook it, the entire house smells of dried fish, at least for a couple of days. I usually cook it outside my house on a butane burner, but, frankly, I love this smell!

Serves: **4** | Time to prepare: **30 minutes** | Store: **Refrigerator, for 2 days**

Ingredients

2 cups dried shrimp
2 Tablespoons vegetable oil
1 cup red onion, minced
¼ jalapeño, minced
¼ teaspoon cayenne powder
½ teaspoon turmeric powder
½ teaspoon salt

Instructions

1. In a 3-qt. sauté pan over medium heat, sauté dried shrimp for 5 minutes. Stir once every minute. Remove from pan and pour into another dish, set aside.
2. Heat oil in the same sauté pan and add jalapeño and onions. Sauté for 10 minutes, stirring once every minute.
3. Once the dried shrimp has somewhat cooled, crumble gently with your hands.
4. Add the remaining ingredients along with shrimp to the sauté pan. Add 2 tablespoons water.
5. Reduce heat to low and cook covered for 10 minutes. Stir once after 5 minutes. Serve.

Green Fish Curry
Hirwi Machchi Rassa

I have not had a fish made with chutney at any restaurant in the US. Sometimes Mummy will make this curry with shrimp, sometimes with chicken. With chicken, you will need to cook this curry longer.

Serves: **4** | Time to prepare: **30 minutes** | Store: **Refrigerator, for 2 days**

Ingredients

2 Tablespoons vegetable oil
1 cup red onion, minced

Marinade:
 1 lb. swordfish fillet, chopped in 2"
 pieces
 1 Tablespoon ginger, minced
 1 Tablespoon peeled garlic, minced
 ½ jalapeño, finely chopped

Chutney:
 1 bunch cilantro, rinsed and roughly
 chopped (use the stalk as well)
 1 bunch mint; pick the leaves off and
 discard the stem; roughly chop
 leaves
 ½ cup regular coconut milk mixed
 with ½ cup water
 2 teaspoons curry powder
 Salt, to taste

Instructions

1. In a mixing bowl, mix the fish along with marinade ingredients. Set aside.
2. In a 3-qt. medium sauté pan over medium heat, heat oil and sauté onions until light brown in color. This should take about 7–8 minutes. Stir every minute.
3. Meanwhile, blend the chutney ingredients to a smooth paste. Add coconut milk first to the blender and add the herbs in 2 or 3 batches.
4. Once the onions are done, add fish along with its marinade and sauté for 5 minutes, stirring gently every minute.
5. Add curry powder and mix. Cook for a minute.
6. Add chutney. Lower heat and cook covered for 15 minutes, stirring gently every 5 minutes. Add salt and serve.

Mummy's Shrimp Curry

Prawn Masala

Mummy makes this recipe once a month. This preparation of shrimp is the most delicious preparation of shrimp I have ever had in my life, so thank you, Mummy, for this.

Serves: **4** | Time to prepare: **60 minutes** | Store: **Refrigerator, for 2 days**

Ingredients

4 Tablespoons oil
2 bay leaves
3 cloves
1 cinnamon stick
1½ cups red onion, minced
1 Tablespoon ginger, minced
1 Tablespoon minced garlic
2 cups Roma tomatoes, chopped
2 Tablespoons curry powder
1 teaspoon cayenne powder
1 teaspoon *garam masala*
1 lb. shrimp, 16–20 count, raw, peeled and deveined
1 cup frozen green peas
1 Tablespoon fresh grated coconut OR 1 Tablespoon regular coconut milk
Salt, to taste
2 Tablespoons chopped cilantro

Instructions

1. In a 3-qt. sauce-pan over medium heat, heat oil.
2. When the oil is hot, add bay leaves, cloves, and cinnamon stick. Sauté for 2 minutes.
3. Add onions and mix, cook for 15 minutes, stirring every 3 minutes.
4. Add ginger and garlic, cook for 5 minutes.
5. Add tomatoes and mix; cook covered for 8 minutes, stirring once after 4 minutes.
6. Add spice powders and mix well. Cook for 2 minutes.
7. Add 1 cup water and bring to a boil.
8. Add shrimp and green peas, mix gently and add ½ cup of water or more, if required.
9. Cook covered for 10 minutes. Stir once after 5 minutes.
10. Add coconut milk, salt, and garnish with cilantro. Serve with rice.

Simple Chicken Curry
Masala Murg

This recipe is perfect for a beginner who is learning how to cook chicken curry. Even though the curry is pretty simple, the result is a tangy and tasty chicken curry.

Serves: **4** | Time to prepare: **45 minutes** | Store: **Refrigerator, for 2 days**

Ingredients

1 lb. boneless skinless chicken thighs, chopped in 2" cubes
1 cup red onion, minced
1 inch ginger, peeled and finely chopped
3–4 garlic cloves, peeled and finely chopped
½ cup whole milk plain yogurt
1 cup Roma tomatoes, finely chopped
2 Tablespoons curry powder
½ teaspoon cayenne powder
1 teaspoon *garam masala* powder
4 Tablespoons vegetable oil
Salt, to taste
1 Tablespoon freshly squeezed lemon juice
2 Tablespoons chopped cilantro

Instructions

1. In a mixing bowl, mix all chicken along with onion, ginger, garlic, yogurt, tomatoes, curry powder, cayenne powder, *garam masala* powder, and 1 teaspoon salt. Mix well and set aside.

2. In a 3-qt. pan over medium heat, heat oil. When the oil is hot, add chicken along with its marinade CAREFULLY into the hot oil. Mix. Cook on high heat for 10 minutes, stirring every other minute.

3. Reduce heat to low and add 1 cup water. Cook covered for 30 minutes on low heat. Stir once every 10 minutes.

4. Adjust salt, squeeze lemon juice, and garnish with cilantro. Serve hot.

Ground Lamb & Peas Curry

Keema Matar

'*Keema*' is ground meat (usually ground up goat meat) and '*matar*' is green peas. This is a semi-dry curry from the north of India. Once again, lamb and fresh mint make a classic combination, and green peas add the freshness and just a little sweet taste to this curry.

Serves: **4** | Time to prepare: **30 minutes** | Store: **Refrigerator, for 3–4 days**

Ingredients

1 lb. ground lamb
2 Tablespoons oil
1 cup red onion, minced
1 Tablespoon fresh ginger, finely chopped
1 Tablespoon peeled garlic, finely chopped
1 cup Roma tomatoes, finely chopped
Spice Mix:
  2 Tablespoons curry powder
  ½ teaspoon cayenne powder
  1 teaspoon paprika powder
  1 teaspoon *garam masala* powder
½ cup mint leaves, chopped
1 cup green peas, preferably frozen and thawed
Salt, to taste

Instructions

1. In a medium-size mixing bowl, add ground lamb and one cup of water. Knead the water into the ground lamb. This will ensure there are no knots when lamb is being cooked. Set aside.
2. In a 3-qt. sauce pan over medium heat, heat oil. Add onions and sauté for 10 minutes or until onions have caramelized. Stir every minute.
3. Add ginger and garlic, cook for 5 minutes, stir once.
4. Add tomatoes and stir, cook for 4–5 minutes, stirring every other minute. When you stir, mash tomatoes with the back of your spoon so that they pulp down.
5. Add spice powders and mix. Then add ground lamb and mix well. Cook for 15 minutes, stirring every 5 minutes. Make sure there are no lumps while the lamb is cooking. Break lumps, if any.
6. Add mint, peas, and salt. Mix. Taste for salt and adjust if needed. Cook for another 5 minutes. Serve.

Mutton Curry

Mutton Rassaywaala

'Mutton' is usually used for goat meat. The key to making goat meat curry is to pressure-cook it or to cook it for a long period of time. The curry is said to be done when the meat falls off the bone. In the US, I use boneless lamb meat instead and cook it for 90 minutes or until the meat is easily broken with a fork.

Serves: **4** | Time to prepare: **120 minutes** | Store: **Refrigerator, for 3–4 days**

Ingredients

1½ lb. boneless skinless lamb shoulder, chopped into 2" cubes
¼ cup oil
1 cinnamon stick
2 dried bay leaves
3 cloves
3 green cardamoms, crushed
1 black cardamom
4–5 black peppercorns
2 cups red onions, thinly sliced
1 Tablespoon fresh ginger, grated
1 Tablespoon peeled garlic, grated
2 cups Roma tomatoes, chopped
2 Tablespoons chopped cilantro

Spice Mix.
2 Tablespoons curry powder
½ teaspoon cayenne powder
1 teaspoon paprika powder
1 teaspoon *garam masala*

Instructions

1. In a 5-qt. sauté pan over medium heat, heat oil. When the oil is hot, add cinnamon, green cardamoms, black cardamoms, bay leaves, cloves, peppercorns, and onions. Sauté for 15 minutes, stirring once every minute.
2. Increase heat to high. Add lamb, ginger and garlic and sauté for 15 minutes. Stir once every 5 minutes.
3. Reduce heat to medium. Add tomatoes and spice mix. Sauté for 5 minutes.
4. Add 3 cups water and bring to a boil. Reduce heat to low, and cover and cook for 90 minutes. Stir every 15 minutes. If the curry needs water, then add ¼ cup at a time.
5. Add salt. If the curry is runny, then remove lid and boil for 10 minutes to thicken it; if not, garnish with chopped cilantro.

INDIAN COOKING FROM MY MOM

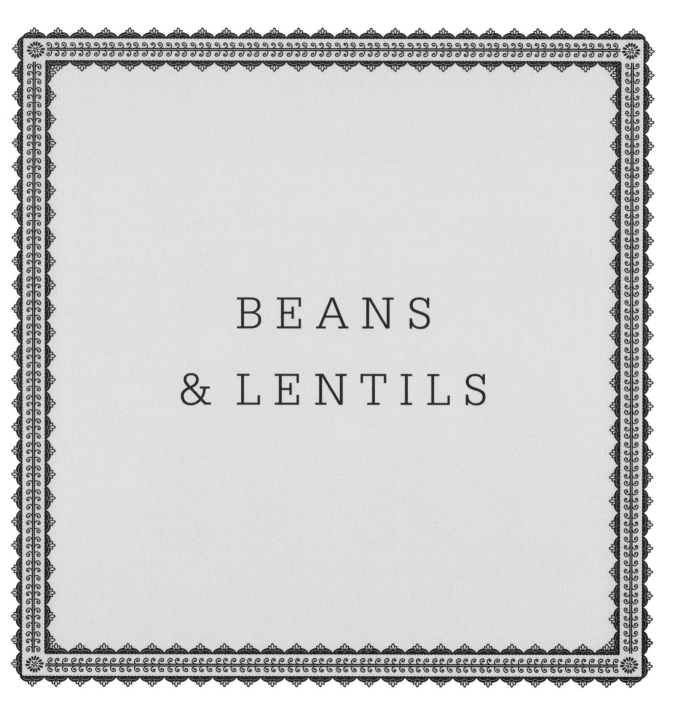

BEANS
& LENTILS

Usage, Storage and Preparation

USAGE:

The world of lentils and beans is a beautiful one. Lentils and beans come in a large array of shapes, sizes, colors, flavors, and textures. Indian cooking makes the best use of all types of lentils and beans. Owing to the fact that Indian cuisine is primarily vegetarian, lentils and beans are the bases for our source of protein. Lentils and beans are inexpensive, without fat and cholesterol, and therefore extremely healthy.

STORAGE:

When you buy dried, raw lentils and beans, store them in air-tight containers; no refrigeration is required. Consume within one year. Once cooked, lentils and beans can be stored in the refrigerator and should be consumed within 3–4 days.

PREPARATION:

How to prepare Beans?

Beans are bought dry rather than as canned beans that contain preservatives and chemicals. One cup of dry, raw beans will yield about 2½ cups of cooked beans. Rinse beans a couple of times under cold running water. Pour beans in a medium-size mixing bowl and add 2 cups of water. Soak for 8 hours. Discard the water in which the beans were soaked (use it to water house plants). Add 2 cups of fresh water and pour all of this in a pressure cooker and cook according to the manufacturer's directions. If you do not own a pressure cooker, then add 4 cups water to a 5-qt. sauté pan. Bring this mixture to a boil. Reduce heat to low and cook covered for 90 minutes.

How to prepare Lentils?

As opposed to beans, lentils are usually split, and will require no soaking beforehand. Sometimes lentils may have skin on them, but they will be split, so even then they don't require any soaking prior to cooking. Rinse lentils just once under cold running water. Usually in a pressure cooker, we add 3 times the water for cooking lentils. If you are not using a pressure cooker, then you will add 4 times the water and cook longer. Recipes in this section describe how to cook lentils with each type of preparation.

Basic Lentils

Serves: **4** | Time to prepare: **60 minutes without a pressure cooker**

Ingredients

1 cup split pigeon peas
(*toor dal*), rinsed

Seasoning:
2 Tablespoons *ghee*
2 pinches *hing*
(asafetida powder)
(OPTIONAL)
1 teaspoon salt OR as
desired
1 Tablespoon sugar
1 teaspoon turmeric
powder
1 teaspoon cumin seeds

Instructions

1. Add all the ingredients in a pressure cooker with 3 cups water. Pressure cook as per manufacturer's directions. If you are not using a pressure cooker, then mix all the ingredients with 4 cups water in a 5-qt. pot with a lid. Bring it to a boil. Once boiling, cover the pot with a lid, reduce heat to simmer, and cook for approximately an hour, or until the lentils have cooked thoroughly.
2. When serving, pour lentils on white basmati rice and top with *ghee*.

Sweet & Sour Lentils
Ambat Goad Varan

This lentil is a staple in our family. The key is to use *goad masala* powder, which is a local version of *garam masala* and *amsul* (a dried sour fruit used as a souring agent).

Serves: **4** | Time to prepare: **60 minutes without a pressure cooker** |
Store: **Refrigerator, for 3–4 days**

Ingredients

1 cup split pigeon peas, rinsed
½ cup peanuts, without skin
½ teaspoon turmeric powder

Seasoning:
2 Tablespoons *ghee*
1 teaspoon cumin seeds
½ jalapeño, finely chopped
4–5 curry leaves, each broken in
  half
4–5 pieces of *amsul* (if you don't
  have *amsul*, substitute with 1
  Tablespoon tamarind pulp)
1 teaspoon *goad masala* powder OR
  garam masala powder
¼ cup fresh grated coconut and ½
cup cilantro, finely chopped
1 Tablespoon *jaggery* OR sugar
Salt, to taste

Instructions

1. In a medium-size pressure cooker, cook lentils in 3 cups water as per manufacturer's directions. If you do not own a pressure cooker, then in a 5-qt. pot with a lid, add lentils and 4 cups of water and bring to a boil. Simmer and cook covered for 1 hour. If lentils are not yet cooked, then add another cup of water and cook for approximately 30 minutes more. You will know that the lentils are cooked when you pick a couple of pieces and break them with your fingers; there should be no powdery white substance in the lentil.
2. Meanwhile, in a small fry pan, melt *ghee* over medium heat. When the *ghee* is hot, add cumin, jalapeño, curry leaves, *amsul*, and *goad masala*. Sauté for 4 minutes.
3. Add turmeric powder, lentils, and salt. Bring it to a boil. Add coconut and cilantro. Cook for approximately 5 minutes, and serve.

Tomato Lentils
Tamatar Dal

At home, this is our favorite lentil. Everyone loves it, and it's easy to prepare.

Serves: **4** | Time to prepare: **60 minutes** | Store: **Refrigerator, for 3–4 days**

Ingredients

1 cup split pigeon peas, rinsed

Seasoning:
2 Tablespoons *ghee*
2 pinches *hing* (asafetida powder)
½ teaspoon black mustard seeds
1 teaspoon cumin seeds
3–4 garlic cloves, minced
½ jalapeño, finely chopped
6 curry leaves, each torn in two pieces (OPTIONAL)
¾ cup Roma tomatoes, chopped
½ teaspoon turmeric powder
¼ teaspoon cayenne powder
1 Tablespoon *jaggery* OR white granulated sugar
Salt, to taste

Instructions

1. In a medium-size pressure cooker, cook lentils in 3 cups water as per manufacturer's directions. If you do not own a pressure cooker, then in a 5-qt. pot with a lid, add lentils and 4 cups of water bring to a boil. Simmer and cook covered for 1 hour; if lentils are not yet cooked, then add another cup of water and cook for another 30 minutes approximately. You will know that the lentils are cooked when you pick a couple of pieces and break them with your fingers and there is no powdery white substance inside the lentil.
2. Meanwhile, in a small fry pan, melt *ghee* over medium heat. When the *ghee* is hot, add *hing* and mustard seeds. Allow seeds to crackle.
3. Add cumin seeds, garlic, jalapeño, and curry leaves. Sauté for 3 minutes. Add ground spices.
4. Add tomatoes and mix. Cook for 5 minutes.
5. Add this mixture to cooked lentils. Then add salt and *jaggery*. Cook for approximately 10 minutes, then garnish with chopped cilantro and serve hot.

Chickpea Curry
Cholay

Cholay or Chickpea curry is extremely popular. It tastes best when you use fresh chickpeas, even though canned chickpeas are rather convenient. Mummy makes *pooris* (fried bread) to go with this curry, a traditional combination.

Serves: **4** | Time to prepare: **30 minutes with pre-cooked beans** |
Store: **Refrigerator, for 3–4 days**

Ingredients

3 Tablespoons light oil
1 cup red onion, minced
2 cups cooked garbanzo beans
1 Tablespoon ginger, minced
1 Tablespoon peeled garlic,
    minced
4 large Roma tomatoes,
    chopped

Spice mix:
1 Tablespoon curry powder
1 teaspoon *garam masala*
    powder
½ teaspoon mango powder
    (IMPORTANT INGREDIENT!)
¼ teaspoon cayenne powder
Salt, to taste
2 Tablespoons chopped cilantro

Instructions

1. In a 3-qt. pot, heat oil for a minute over medium heat. Add onions and sauté for 5–10 minutes, stirring every couple of minutes until onions are just about brown.
2. Add ginger and garlic; mix well and sauté for approximately 2 minutes, stirring every minute.
3. Add tomatoes, mix, and cook covered on low heat for approximately 5 minutes, stirring every minute.
4. Add the spice powders and mix well. Sauté for a minute. Mash tomatoes with the back of your stirring spoon to pulp tomatoes.
5. Add ½ cup water and garbanzo beans. Mix well. Bring the mixture to a boil over medium heat, adjust salt. Cover and cook for approximately 15 minutes.
6. Use the back of your stirring spoon to mash garbanzo beans partially. Garnish with cilantro.

Red Kidney Beans
Rajma

Serves: **4** | Time to prepare: **30 minutes with pre-cooked beans** |
Store: **Refrigerator, for 3–4 days**

Ingredients

2 cups cooked red kidney beans
(see 'preparation' section on
cooking red kidney beans)
3 Tablespoons light oil
1 Tablespoon cumin seeds
1 cup red onion, finely chopped
1 Tablespoon fresh ginger, peeled
and grated
1 Tablespoon fresh garlic cloves,
peeled and grated
1½ cups Roma tomatoes, finely
chopped
1 Tablespoon coriander powder
1 teaspoon *garam masala*
¼ teaspoon cayenne powder
Salt, to taste
1 Tablespoon plain whole milk
yogurt (OPTIONAL)
2 Tablespoons chopped cilantro

Instructions

1. In a 5-qt. sauté pan, heat oil over medium heat. When the oil is hot, add cumin seeds and sauté for half a minute.
2. Add onions, mix, and sauté for 8 minutes or until onions have started to caramelize. Stir every minute.
3. Add ginger and garlic. Sauté for approximately 5 minutes, stirring every minute.
4. Add tomatoes, mix, and cook covered for approximately 5 minutes.
5. Add ground spices and mash tomatoes, using the back of your stirring spoon.
6. When the tomatoes have been mashed, add beans and 1 cup water. Bring to a boil.
7. Add some salt, and cook for approximately 15 minutes over medium heat.
8. Use the back of your spatula to mash half of the beans. Add yogurt, garnish with cilantro, and mix.

Black-eyed Peas Curry
Chawli

Black-eyed peas require no soaking, unlike peas or beans. Mummy makes this sweet-and-sour recipe with dried black-eyed peas, but you can always use pre-cooked, frozen black-eyed peas. In this recipe, I am using pre-cooked, frozen black-eyed peas.

Serves: **4** | Time to prepare: **30 minutes** | Store: **Refrigerator, for 3–4 days**

Ingredients

2 cups pre-cooked, frozen black-eyed peas
2 Tablespoons light oil
1 teaspoon cumin seeds
½ cup red onion, finely chopped
1 cup Roma tomatoes, chopped
1 teaspoon coriander powder
¼ teaspoon cayenne powder
½ teaspoon turmeric powder
½ teaspoon *garam masala*
½ teaspoon mango powder
1 Tablespoon *jaggery* OR ½ Tablespoon white granulated sugar
Salt, to taste

Instructions

1. In a 3-qt. pot over medium heat, heat oil and add cumin seeds. Sauté for a minute.
2. Add onions and cook until onions begin to caramelize or for approximately 10 minutes, stirring every minute. Then add tomatoes and cook for approximately 10 minutes. Stir once after 5 minutes.
3. Add ground spices and mix. Cook for approx. 2 minutes.
4. Add peas along with 1 cup water and bring to a boil. Once the peas have come to a boil, lower heat to medium-low and cook until they have been cooked. You will know that the peas are cooked when you pick a couple of them and press them and they feel soft, not grainy.
5. Add salt and *jaggery*, stir, and serve.

Note: If you are unable to find mango powder, use 1 tablespoon of lemon juice instead.

Split Yellow Mung Lentils
Mung Dal

Serves: **4** | Time to prepare: **30 minutes** | Store: **Refrigerator, for 3–4 days**

Mung lentils are considered to have a good amount of protein, especially good for people who cannot digest heavy meat protein. These yellow lentils require no soaking.

Ingredients

1 cup split yellow mung lentils, rinsed
2 Tablespoons oil
½ teaspoon black mustard seeds
1 teaspoon cumin seeds
3–4 garlic cloves, finely chopped
½ cup red onion, finely chopped
½ cup Roma tomatoes, finely chopped
¼ teaspoon cayenne powder
½ teaspoon turmeric powder
Salt, to taste
2 Tablespoons chopped cilantro

Instructions

1. In a 3-qt. pot, add lentils with 3 cups of water and bring to a boil. Once boiling, cover and cook on simmer for 25 minutes.
2. Meanwhile, in a small fry pan, heat oil over medium heat.
3. Add mustard seeds and allow crackling.
4. Add cumin seeds and sauté for 30 seconds. Add garlic and cook for approximately 5 minutes.
5. Add onions and sauté for approximately 10 minutes, stirring every minute.
6. Add tomatoes and mix. Cook for approximately 2 minutes. Then add all spice powders.
7. Add this mixture to the cooked lentils and stir. Add salt and bring the mixture to a boil over medium heat. Garnish with cilantro. Serve.

Sprouted Mung Beans Curry
Matth ki Usal

Serves: **4** | Time to prepare: **45 minutes**| Store: **Refrigerator, for 3–4 days**

Mummy buys whole green mung beans, soaks them in water and then ties the beans in cheesecloth. She places these in a mixing bowl and adds a cup of water. She then places the bowl in the sun. In about 2 days, the beans will have sprouted. (She adds another cup of water if the bowl start to dry out.) Simple pleasures of a tropical climate!

Ingredients

2 cups sprouted green mung beans
2 Tablespoons oil
½ teaspoon black mustard seeds
1 teaspoon cumin seeds
½ jalapeño, finely chopped
½ cup red onion, finely chopped
1inch fresh ginger, peeled and
   grated
2 garlic cloves, peeled and grated
1 Tablespoon curry powder
1 teaspoon *garam masala*
Salt, to taste

Garnish:
2 Tablespoons dry unsweetened
   coconut
2 Tablespoons cilantro, chopped

Instructions

1. In a 3-qt. sauté pan over medium heat, heat oil and add black mustard seeds. Allow them to crackle.
2. Add cumin and jalapeño and sauté for approx. 2 minutes. Then add onions and cook for approx. 7 minutes, stirring once every minute.
3. Add ginger and garlic and cook for approx. 5 minutes.
4. Add curry powder and *garam masala*, cook for a minute.
5. Add sprouted mung beans and salt, as desired. Mix. Add 1 cup of water and mix.
6. Reduce heat to low, cover and cook for 25 minutes, stirring once every 5 minutes.
7. Garnish with cilantro and coconut and mix. Serve.

INDIAN COOKING FROM MY MOM

Split Garbanzo Lentils
Chanay ki Dal

Split garbanzo lentils are the inside of garbanzo beans; they are sold dried and split. They take longer to cook, perhaps the longest in the world of lentils. I make these lentils with an East Indian recipe from the Indian state of Bengal, but here is Mummy's recipe.

Serves: **4** | Time to prepare: **60 minutes** | Store: **Refrigerator, for 3–4 days**

Ingredients

1 cup split garbanzo lentils
2 Tablespoons oil
½ teaspoon black mustard seeds
1 teaspoon cumin seeds
½ jalapeño, finely chopped
½ cup red onion, finely chopped
1 inch fresh ginger, peeled and grated
2 garlic cloves, peeled and grated
1 teaspoon dried mango powder (OPTIONAL)
1 Tablespoon curry powder
1 teaspoon *garam masala*
Salt, to taste

Instructions

1. In a 3-qt. sauté pan, add 3 cups water and lentils. Bring to a boil.
2. Cover with a lid, reduce heat to simmer, and cook for 1 hour.
3. Meanwhile, in a 3-qt. sauté pan over medium heat, heat oil and add black mustard seeds. Allow them to crackle.
4. Add cumin and jalapeño and sauté for approx. 2 minutes. Then add onions and cook for approx. 5 minutes, stirring once every minute.
5. Add ginger and garlic and cook for 2 minutes.
6. Add mango powder, curry powder, and *garam masala*. Cook for a minute.
7. Add cooked lentils and salt as desired. Mix. Add 1 cup of water and mix.
8. Reduce heat to low, cover, and cook for approx. 15 minutes, stirring once every 5 minutes.

Whole French Lentils

Kali Masoor

Black whole French lentils are French lentils before they are split. Since they are whole and have a layer of covering, they take much longer to cook.

Serves: **4** | Time to prepare: **60 minutes** | Store: **Refrigerator, for 3–4 days**

Ingredients

1 cup whole French lentils
2 Tablespoons oil
½ cup red onion, finely
    chopped
1 cup Roma tomatoes, finely
    chopped
1 Tablespoon coriander
    powder
¼ teaspoon cayenne powder
½ teaspoon turmeric powder
½ teaspoon *garam masala*
    powder
Salt, to taste

Instructions

1. In a medium-size pressure cooker, cook lentils in 3 cups water as per manufacturer's directions. If you do not own a pressure cooker, then in a 5-qt. pot with a lid, add lentils and 4 cups of water and bring to a boil. Simmer and cook, covered, for 1 hour. If lentils are not yet cooked, then add another cup of water and cook for another 30 minutes. You will know that the lentils are cooked when you pick a couple of pieces and break them with your fingers and no powdery white substance is observed inside the lentil.
2. Meanwhile, in a small fry pan, heat oil.
3. Add onions and sauté for approx. 10 minutes, stirring every minute.
4. Add tomatoes and mix. Cook for 5 minutes.
5. Add spice powders and mix. Cook for 2 minutes. Add this mixture to the cooked lentils.
6. Add salt and mix. Bring to a boil. Mash some of the lentils with the back of your stirring spoon. Serve.

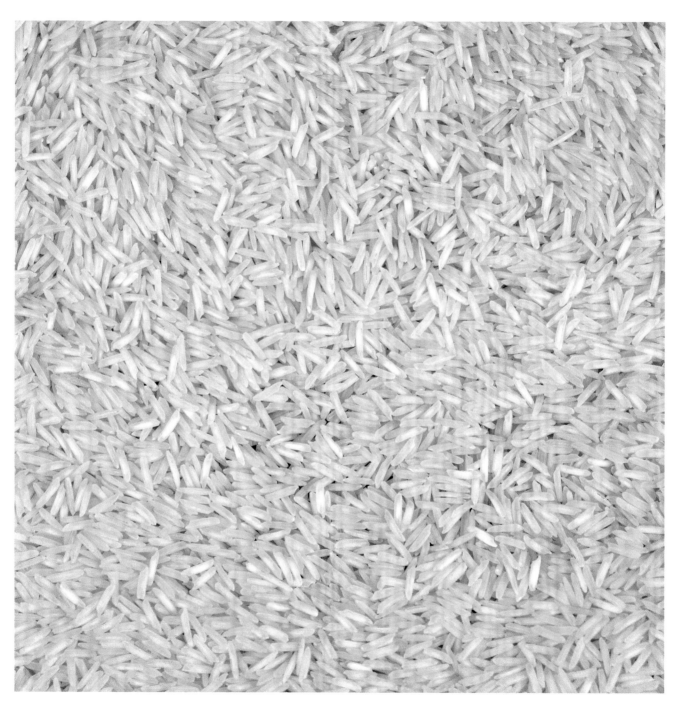

BREADS & RICE

Unleavened Wheat Bread

Roti

Roti is unleavened bread that, in the USA, can be made with 100% whole wheat white flour. It is always made fresh and served warm during a meal. I remember when my mom used to go on vacation and I had to make *roti*s for my dog; he used to never eat them since I rolled them unevenly and they didn't puff up in the cooking. He was a family member and brought a lot of happiness, may his soul rest in peace.

Serves: **4** | Total time: **60 minutes**. Active time: **30 minutes** | Store: **Refrigerator, for 7 days**

Ingredients
2 cups (plus ¼ cup) 100% whole wheat white flour

Instructions

1. In a mixing bowl, add flour and ½ cup water. Knead soft dough with your hands. You will need more water; add 2 Tablespoons at a time. Set aside for 30 minutes.
2. Take a small piece of the dough, roll in your palms and flatten it.
3. Roll a 6" disc (¼" thick). Use flour to dust the surface before you roll the dough into a disc. Prepare discs similarly. Heat a medium fry pan over medium heat.
4. Dust excess flour from disc and place it carefully on the fry pan. Cook it for 3 minutes.
5. Using a pair of tongs, flip it and cook the other side for 3 minutes.
6. Remove fry pan from heat, increase heat to high and, using a pair of tongs, place the *roti* directly on heat for about 15 seconds. *Roti* should puff up; this is an indicator that the *roti* has been prepared correctly. Remove from heat and place it on a plate.
7. Prepare and cook the remaining discs in the same manner. Serve.

Chickpea Pancakes
Chilay

Mummy makes these pancakes for breakfast. They are rich in protein as they are made from chickpea flour. At home, she typically serves them with tomato ketchup and *chai*.

Serves: **8** | Time to prepare: **45 minutes** | Store: **Refrigerator, for 3–4 days**

Ingredients

2 cups chickpea flour
½ cup red onion, minced
1 Tablespoon cumin seeds
½ cup Roma tomatoes, finely
  chopped
1 Tablespoon cilantro, finely
  chopped
½ teaspoon turmeric powder
½ teaspoon cayenne powder
1 teaspoon salt
¼ cup vegetable oil

Instructions

1. In a mixing bowl, add flour and 1 cup water. Mix for a couple of minutes so that there are no lumps in the batter. As required, you can keep adding more water (a little at a time) to make a batter that has a pancake-batter consistency.
2. Add remaining ingredients except oil and mix again. Set aside for 10 minutes.
3. Meanwhile, heat a medium non-stick fry pan over medium heat and pour in half a teaspoon of oil.
4. Pour 1/3 cup of batter into pan and spread to form a pancake. Cook for 3-4 minutes. Add ½ teaspoon oil around the sides of the pancake.
5. Use a spatula and flip the pancake, cook the other side for 2 minutes. Remove and serve. Repeat the last 3 steps for the remaining batter.

INDIAN COOKING FROM MY MOM

White Basmati Rice
Chawal

Cooking white basmati rice is quite different from cooking any other rice. Since this rice is not fortified, it must be rinsed. Rice is rinsed by placing it in a medium-size mixing bowl and rinsing it 3 times with double the water, you must drain the water each time rice is rinsed and then repeat the process. Make sure that you do not waste grains of rice during this process. Once the rice has been rinsed, keep it aside for 15-20 minutes. This will ensure longer grains. The rice is now ready for cooking.

Ingredients

1 cup white basmati rice, rinsed as mentioned above

Instructions

A few different ways to cook rice:

1. In a rice cooker: Cook white basmati rice as per manufacturer's directions.
2. Low-starch rice: In a pasta pot, add rinsed white basmati rice and 6 cups of water and pour in a pot. Bring it to a boil on medium high heat. Keep cooking until rice grains have been cooked. You will need to test this by pressing a couple of rice grains and making sure that they are not hard. Rice will turn soft once cooked. Strain the water using a mesh.
3. Rice in a pot: Add rice to a medium-sized pot along with double the quantity of water. Bring it to a boil; then cook covered on low heat until all the water is absorbed. 1 cup of raw rice should be cooked in about 15 minutes or when all the water has been absorbed by the rice.

Rice and Lentil preparation
Khichadi

There are many recipes for making *khichadi*. It can be as simple as my mom's recipe below, or you can add many vegetables and spices to it. *Khichadi* is a good combination of carbohydrates and protein in one dish, and hence a complete meal in itself.

Serves: **4** | Time to prepare: **45 minutes** | Store: **Refrigerator, for 3–4 days**

Ingredients

3 Tablespoons *ghee*
1 Tablespoon cumin seeds
1 cup white basmati rice OR
  any other white rice
1 cup split mung lentils (either
  with skin-on or skinless)
1 teaspoon salt
1 jalapeño, finely chopped
¼ cup chopped cilantro

Instructions

1. In a medium mixing bowl, add rice and lentils.
2. Then add 4 cups water and mix. Rinse.
3. Drain water and set aside for 15 minutes.
4. In a pressure cooker, melt *ghee* over medium heat. When the *ghee* has melted, add cumin seeds and jalapeño, and sauté for 2 minutes.
5. Add rice and lentils and 1 teaspoon salt.
6. Add 5 cups water and pressure cook as per manufacturer's directions. Serve.

Note:
If you do not have a pressure cooker, then after you have added 5 cups water, bring the mixture to a boil. Once the mixture has come to a boil, reduce heat to simmer and cook covered for 30 minutes or until all water has been absorbed by rice and lentils. Serve.

Royal Pulao

A simple flavorful rice dish with a lot of nuts. In Indian cooking, we use almonds, cashew nuts and golden raisins when using dried fruits.

Serves: **4** | Time to prepare: **45 minutes** | Store: **Refrigerator, for 3–4 days**

Ingredients

2 Tablespoons *ghee*
1 cup thinly sliced red onion
1 dried bay leaf
3 cloves
3 green cardamom pods, partially crushed
1 cinnamon stick, broken into two
6 almonds, thinly sliced
6 cashew nuts, each broken into two – lengthwise
12 golden raisins
½ teaspoon *garam masala* powder
1 cup white basmati rice
Salt, to taste
2 Tablespoons cilantro, garnish

Instructions

1. In a 5-qt. wide-bottom sauté pan, melt *ghee* over medium heat.
2. Add onions, cloves, cinnamon, cardamom and bay leaves. Mix. Cook for 10 minutes, stirring every minute.
3. Add nuts and sauté for 5 minutes, stirring every minute.
4. Meanwhile, in a medium mixing bowl, add rice and rinse it 3 times under cold running water. Make sure not to waste any rice grains. Drain excess water each time.
5. Add this rice to the pan along with 2 cups water and *garam masala* powder. Add 1 teaspoon salt. Bring the mixture to a boil.
6. Reduce heat to simmer and cook, covered, for 12 minutes, or until all water has been absorbed by rice. Garnish with cilantro and serve.

Tomato & Fenugreek Pulao

Tamatar aur Methi Pulao

My sister-in-law taught us how to make this rice. It is a very simple and flavorful dish.

Ingredients

1½ cups white basmati rice
2 Tablespoons *ghee*
1 Tablespoon cumin seeds
½ cup dried fenugreek
  leaves
2 cups Roma tomatoes,
  finely chopped
Salt, to taste

Instructions

1. Add rice to a medium mixing bowl and rinse 3 times under cold water. Drain water and make sure that you do not waste rice grains while rinsing rice. Set aside.
2. Meanwhile, in a 5-qt. wide-bottom pot over medium heat, melt *ghee*. When the *ghee* has melted, add cumin seeds and sauté for a minute.
3. Add fenugreek leaves and sauté for a minute. Add tomatoes, mix and cook for 5 minutes, stirring once after 3 minutes.
4. Add rice and 2½ cups water. Bring to a boil.
5. Reduce heat to simmer and cook, covered, until all water has been absorbed by rice. This should take about 15–20 minutes.

Cumin-flavored Rice

Ingredients

2 Tablespoons *ghee*
1 Tablespoon cumin seeds
½ cup frozen green peas
2 cups cooked basmati rice
Salt, to taste

Instructions

1. In a large fry pan, heat *ghee* over medium heat.
2. Add cumin seeds, salt and peas. Sauté for 2 minutes.
3. Add rice and mix gently; make sure you are not breaking any rice grains while mixing.

Both rice: Serves: **4** | Time to prepare: **45 minutes**| Store: **Refrigerator, for 3 days**

Lemon Rice
Rice seasoned with spices and lemon juice

Lemon Rice is quite popular in our home in Mumbai. We make this with leftover rice, most likely prepared the day before. Similar to this rice, you can make coconut rice, tamarind rice and yogurt rice, with some minor variations to this recipe.

Serves: **4** | Time to prepare: **15 minutes** | Store: **Refrigerator, for 3–4 days**

Ingredients

2 Tablespoons *ghee*
1 teaspoon black mustard seeds
1 teaspoon cumin seeds
1 dry chili, torn into two pieces
5–6 curry leaves, each torn into
    two pieces
½ cup red onion, finely chopped
½ teaspoon turmeric powder
2 cups cooked white basmati rice
1 teaspoon white granulated sugar
Salt, to taste
2 Tablespoons freshly squeezed
    lemon juice
½ cup cilantro, finely chopped

Instructions

1. In a large fry pan, heat *ghee* over medium heat.
2. Add mustard seeds and allow crackling.
3. Add cumin seeds, dry red chilies, onions and curry leaves. Sauté for 5 minutes.
4. Add turmeric powder and sauté for 30 seconds.
5. Add rice, sugar and ½ teaspoon salt. Stir gently; make sure you are not breaking rice grains while mixing rice with other ingredients in the fry pan.
6. Add lemon juice and cilantro, toss and serve.

Coconut Rice
Rice seasoned with spices and coconut

Coconut Rice is a South Indian preparation that is very similar to Lemon Rice. You can make this recipe with unsweetened dried coconut or with fresh grated coconut.

Serves: **4** | Time to prepare: **15 minutes** | Store: **Refrigerator, for 3–4 days**

Ingredients

2 Tablespoons *ghee*
1 teaspoon black mustard seeds
1 teaspoon cumin seeds
1 dry chili, torn into two pieces
5–6 curry leaves, each torn into two
  pieces
½ cup red onion, finely chopped
4 cashew nuts, broken into two
2 cups cooked white basmati rice
Salt, to taste
½ cup scraped fresh coconut OR ½
  cup dried unsweetened shredded
  coconut
½ cup cilantro, finely chopped

Instructions

1. In a large fry pan, heat *ghee* over medium heat.
2. Add mustard seeds and allow crackling.
3. Add cumin seeds, dry red chilies, onions and curry leaves. Sauté for 5 minutes.
4. Add cashew nuts and sauté for 30 seconds.
5. Add rice and ½ teaspoon salt. Stir gently; make sure you are not breaking rice grains while mixing rice with other ingredients in the fry pan.
6. Add coconut and cilantro; toss and serve.

Eggplant Pulao
Masalay Bhaat

This is a great dish to make for potlucks, a special dish that looks complicated and involved but is relatively simple. Mummy makes *raita* to go with this recipe.

Serves: **4** | Time to prepare: **45 minutes** | Store: **Refrigerator, for 3–4 days**

Ingredients

1½ cups white basmati rice
2 Tablespoons *ghee*
1 cinnamon stick, broken into two
3 cloves
3 green cardamoms, crushed
1 large dried bay leaf, broken into
    two
2 dry red chilies
1 teaspoon cumin seeds
1 cup red onion, thinly sliced
1 teaspoon *garam masala* powder
2 Tablespoons dried shredded
    coconut
½ teaspoon turmeric powder
2 cups eggplant, chopped into
    1"cubes
Salt, to taste
¼ cup chopped cilantro

Instructions

1. Add rice to a medium mixing bowl and rinse 3 times under cold water. Drain water and make sure that you do not waste rice grains while rinsing rice. Set aside.
2. Meanwhile, in a 5-qt. wide-bottom pot over medium heat, melt *ghee*. When the *ghee* has melted, add cinnamon sticks, cloves, cardamoms, bay leaves, red chilies, cumin seeds and onions. Sauté for 10 minutes. Stir once every other minute.
3. Add coconut, *garam masala*, turmeric and mix. Add eggplant and 1 teaspoon salt. Mix.
4. Add rice and 3 cups water. Bring the mixture to a boil.
5. Reduce heat to simmer and cover with a lid and cook until all water has been absorbed by rice. This should take about 15–20 minutes. Garnish with cilantro and serve.

SWEETS

Golden Sweetened Yogurt
Shrikhand

This is a popular sweet dish that is made by sweetening strained yogurt. For straining yogurt, Mummy prepared the yogurt overnight, strained in a muslin cloth hung over our sink. She collected the whey that dripped from the yogurt and poured it into the soil next day; it has a many nutrients that nourish plant growth. My dad was always assigned the job of beating the yogurt and sugar for preparing this sweet.

Serves: **8** | Time to prepare: **24 hours,** Active time: **30 minutes** |
Store: **Refrigerator, for 7 days**

Ingredients

2 lbs. plain whole milk yogurt, emptied in a cheese cloth, tied up and left hanging over your sink overnight (strained)
1 cup granulated white sugar
3 cardamom pods, finely crushed OR 1 teaspoon cardamom powder

Instructions

1. Once the yogurt has been strained overnight, all the sour water (whey) has left the yogurt. What you have now is thick, non-watery, strained/hung yogurt. If you have used 2 lbs. of whole milk yogurt, it must have reduced to 1/3 its quantity. Empty this yogurt into a mixing bowl and whisk.
2. Add sugar and whisk for about 2 minutes. Set aside for half an hour so that all sugar can dissolve. Add cardamom powder and whisk again for one minute.
3. Refrigerate for 8 hours and serve chilled with hot *pooris* (deep fried bread) or as dessert by itself.

Note: You may garnish with *chironji* (a nut typical to India) or chopped pistachios.

Rice Pudding
Kheer

Ingredients

4 cups whole milk
1 teaspoon saffron
3 Tablespoons white basmati rice, soaked in
 ½ cup water
6 Tablespoons sugar
½ teaspoon cardamom powder
Handful cashew nuts, broken
Handful raisins

Instructions

1. Warm ½ cup milk in a bowl and soak saffron strands in it. Set aside.
2. Boil remaining milk. Once milk comes to a boil, add rice and reduce heat. Cook until the mixture reduces to half the quantity. Stir every couple of minutes.
3. Add sugar. Crush rice partially in the pot itself using the back of your spoon.
4. Add cardamom and saffron along with the milk, cashew nuts, and raisins. Mix. Cook for another 5 minutes on low heat. Serve.

Carrot Pudding
Gajar Ka Halwa

Ingredients

Handful each – cashew nuts, raisins, almonds
3 Tablespoons *ghee*
4 cups grated carrots (grate carrots using a food processor OR a grater)
2 cups evaporated milk
1 cup granulated sugar
¼ teaspoon green cardamom powder

Instructions

1. Roughly chop cashew nuts, raisins, and almonds.
2. Heat ghee over medium heat in a medium pot. Sauté nuts for 2 minutes.
3. Add carrots and sauté for 5 minutes. Stir every minute.
4. Reduce heat to low and add evaporated milk.Cook for about 30 minutes or until carrots have absorbed all milk. Stir every minute.
5. Add sugar and cardamom powder. Mix well.
6. Cook for another 3–4 minutes. Serve hot or at room temperature.

Both puddings: Serves: **4** | Time to prepare: **45 minutes** | Store: **Refrigerator, for 3–4 days**

Sweet Coconut Turnovers
Karanji

At home, Mummy makes this each year for *Diwali* (our most auspicious festival of the year). Instead of puff pastry sheets, she makes all-purpose flour dough and fries these turnovers in *ghee*. This recipe is modified as I like to make it.

Serves: **9** | Time to prepare: **45 minutes** | Store: **Refrigerator, for 7 days**

Ingredients

2 sheets puff pastry, thawed, then each sheet cut in 9 same-size squares and placed in the refrigerator

Filling:

1 cup shredded unsweetened coconut
½ cup sugar
½ teaspoon cardamom powder

Instructions

1. Pre-heat oven at 375° F on bake.
2. Take one pastry sheet square in your palm and place 1 Tablespoon of the filling in the center of the sheet. Wrap the sheet such that the diagonal ends meet and the sheet forms a triangle. Use water to seal the ends if needed or seal without using water.
3. Set aside and similarly prepare remaining sheet squares. Place the triangles on a cookie sheet. Place the cookie sheet in the center of the oven and bake for 20–25 minutes or until the turnovers are light brown in color.
4. Remove from the oven. Let cool for about 10 minutes and serve warm.

INDIAN COOKING FROM MY MOM

Tea-time Coconut Cake
Nariyal Cake

Growing up, we used to get this cake from Mummy's friend, Mary Aunty, every *Diwali*. This is a very simple cake recipe; it is made from fresh coconut (scraped), which is available at most Asian/ Indian ethnic grocery stores. Mary Aunty adds pink food color to this cake, but I refrain from using artificial ingredients. No icing required.

Serves: **8** | Time to prepare: **5 hours**, Active time: **30 minutes** |
Store: **Refrigerator, for 4 days**

Ingredients

3 eggs
1¼ cup semolina
1 cup sugar
2 cups fresh grated coconut
1 cup butter
1 teaspoon baking powder
1 teaspoon vanilla extract

Instructions

1. Beat eggs, sugar, and butter in a mixing bowl. Add the rest of the ingredients and mix well. Set aside for 4 hours.
2. Bake in a 9" diameter pan for 20–25 minutes in a pre-heated oven at 350° F, or until done. Let cool and cut into pieces to serve.

Saffron Sweet Rice

Kesari Bhaat

This dessert is made all over India. In South India it is made with the addition of fresh coconut, or sometimes it is cooked in coconut milk instead of water. The key is to add sugar only after the rice has almost been cooked; otherwise the rice may not cook thoroughly.

Serves: **8** | Time to prepare: **45 minutes** | Store: **Refrigerator, for 3–4 days**

Ingredients

2 Tablespoons *ghee*
4 cloves
1 cinnamon stick, broken into two
1½ cups white basmati rice, rinsed under cold running water
1 cup white granulated sugar
1 teaspoon saffron soaked in ½ cup warm water for 30 minutes
¼ teaspoon cardamom powder
Handful, golden raisins
Handful, unsalted cashew nuts, roughly chopped

Instructions

1. In a 5-qt. sauté pan with a lid, melt *ghee* over medium heat.
2. Add cloves and cinnamon and sauté for 2 minutes.
3. Add rinsed rice and sauté for 5 minutes. Stir every minute, making sure not to break rice grains while stirring.
4. Add 1½ cups water and mix. Reduce heat to simmer and cook, covered, for 15 minutes.
5. Add nuts, sugar, cardamom, and the saffron along with its water. Stir gently.
6. Cook covered for another 15 minutes or until all water has been absorbed by rice. Serve.

Semolina Pudding
Halwa

This semolina pudding, called '*Sheera*' or '*Halwa*,' is served in all temples in India. It is an extremely popular Indian dessert, and no ritual happens without a version of semolina pudding as a dessert. This is a classic version of this dessert.

Serves: **8** | Time to prepare: **45 minutes** | Store: **Refrigerator, for 3 days**

Ingredients

1 cup *ghee*
½ cup golden raisins
½ cup unsalted cashew nuts, partially crushed
1 cup semolina
3 cups whole milk
1 cup sugar
½ teaspoon cardamom powder

Instructions

1. Heat a 3-qt. sauté pan over medium heat and add *ghee*.
2. When *ghee* melts, add nuts and sauté until raisins plump. Remove using a slotted spoon and set aside.
3. Reduce heat to low and add semolina to remaining *ghee* in the pan. Mix and sauté for about 15 minutes or until semolina turns light brown in color. Stir every minute.
4. Add milk and mix. Cook for 2–3 minutes, stirring constantly.
5. Add sugar, cardamom powder, and nuts.
6. Cover partially with a lid and keep stirring.
7. When all the milk has been soaked by semolina, stir every minute for approximately 10 minutes or until *ghee* starts to ooze out of the pudding.
8. Serve hot along with cold vanilla ice cream.

INDIAN COOKING FROM MY MOM

RUPEN RAO

Photo credit: Kingston Kodan
Website: www.KingstonKodan.com

Originally from Mumbai, India, Rupen Rao now resides in Washington, D.C., where he serves as an Indian culinary advisor. Through his 'Simply Indian' cooking classes, Rupen aims to simplify Indian cooking and cuisine for American and international audiences. Rupen has over nine years' experience teaching Indian cooking in the Washington, D.C. Metropolitan area and currently teaches at Whole Foods Market, Living Social's Center at 918 F Street, and at Culinaerie – a premier recreational cooking school. Rupen supplies his own brand of Indian spice mixes to Whole Foods and other specialty stores in Washington, D.C..

For more information on Rupen Rao visit
www.RupenRao.com
Facebook: www.Facebook.com/RupenDC
Twitter: www.Twitter.com/@RupenRao